Written Expressions

Unspoken Truth

Written Expressions
Unspoken Truth

by Anita Vaughn

Christian Literature & Artwork
A BOLD TRUTH Publication

Written Expression
Unspoken Truth
Copyright © 2020 by Anita Vaughn
ISBN 13: 978-1-949993-26-4

FIRST EDITION

BOLD TRUTH PUBLISHING
(Christian Literature & Artwork)
606 West 41st, Ste. 4
Sand Springs, Oklahoma 74063
www.BoldTruthPublishing.com
boldtruthbooks@yahoo.com

Available from Amazon.com and other retail outlets. Orders by U.S. trade bookstores and wholesalers.

Quantity sales special discounts are available on quantity purchases by corporations, associations, and others. For details, contact the publisher at the address above.

Cover Art & Design provided by the Author.

Printed in the USA.
03 20   10 9 8 7 6 5 4 3 2 1

Contents

Contents

Contents

Contents

Contents

Contents

First I give all honor and glory to God. He is the reason that I was able to write this book.

To my parents, Charlie and Norvilene Vaughn, my spiritual counselor, Dr. Velma J. Jones (World Overcomers Ministries), My church family, Vision Outreach Center and My best friend Delisha Tillis Johnson you all have been the best support that anyone could ever ask for. I would not have made it through so much in my life without you. The time you have spent on praying and lifting me up is greatly appreciated. I thank God for you and can never repay you for your worth.

I give a special thanks to my children Treveon Vaughn and Aniesha Vaughn whom I love more than life itself. I strive and live life for you. You are the reason I do what I do. You have seen me laugh, cry, and go through so many levels but not once have you ever doubted my ability to survive and make something of myself.

I know that God will bless each one of you for your commitment to his child.

"The poems you are about to read are from the heart. I've watched the writer go through the Valley of life to the Mountain top of Victory. Being a witness to this transformation was amazing in itself and a testament to those who desire to overcome.

"If you need encouragement you will find it here and know that your current condition isn't your final outcome."

Pastor Marcus Brent Sr.

"Through faith in God's Word, talking and writing therapy is a viable tool to help us effectively navigate the darkest days in life, that we all will inevitably face at some time.

"Anita's success in doing just that is progressively shown throughout the pages of this book. Anita takes us on a journey riddled with emotional pain brought on by all too common circumstances of betrayal, divorce, emotional confusion, and no clear pathway out of the darkness. Through her persistent study of the Word of God and writing her experiences in the light of God's promises, Anita has proven that negative thoughts and hopelessness can be overcome through diligent pursuit of God's Word, prayer, and talking and writing therapy.

"Her writing style is exciting, expressive and enjoyable as she helps her readers sort out their own feelings and build hope for a brighter future."

Dr. Velma Jean Jones

Written Expressions Unspoken Truth has been a journey of life changes, ups and downs, love, hurt, disappointment, joy, loneliness and so much more. It has transformed me from an angry hurt woman to a person of great understanding and forgiveness.

Each poem is written from the heart and what I was personally going through at that time. Through my experiences I want to help others overcome some of the difficulties that they may face on a day to day basis.

I can reflect back on each page and see my life from then to now and be so grateful that God is forever present in my life.

This book has truly made me a better person and I pray that it will bless many others, as it has blessed and changed me.

God Bless,
Anita Vaughn

Section 1

Begin

Section 1

I Miss You Because You Were Mine

I miss your smile, I miss your tender touch,
I miss when you tell me, you love me so much.
I miss your kindness, I miss your love,
I miss that you're not here to share that love.
I miss the good times, I miss the bad times,
It's you I miss, because you were mine.
I miss your open arms, I miss all the fun times too:
You vanished, and left me crying just for you.
I miss our hearts becoming as one,
Sharing our thoughts under the amazing sun.
I miss you and always will.
I miss you; because, you were always there to give.
I miss you; because, you were mine.

Anita Vaughn 1990   Unspoken Truth

Feelings Deep Inside

I have a feeling deep inside of me,

Yelling and screaming, saying: please save me.

It's a feeling of affection to someone so nice and sweet.

My affection was thrown out in the street.

I wish I could express to you, what's all wrapped up inside.

I'm the shy type and hold it all with pride.

This feeling that I have so deep inside, is my love for you.

One day I will get to express my feelings; that are so true.

A Special Love

As I sit and think, all I see,

Are two special people, who are you and me.

A special love, that shines brighter than the sun.

Touches our heart to say, you are the one.

Ups and downs we all must have.

A special love like ours, must put them in the past.

One there for the other and the other for the one,

Gives us a joy of laughter and fun.

A special love, is what I have for you.

My special love, comes from your special love too.

Holding hands, taking strolls through the park.

This is the special love, that comes from the heart.

Anita Vaughn 1991   Unspoken Truth

Sincerely Yours

As I closed my eyes, the tears fell from my face.

I missed you so, especially your warm gentle embrace.

As I slept in this cold lonely bed,

All that went through my mind, was all that was said.

The words said, tore me apart. Then you stomped on my heart.

The apology was given; in sorrow and pain.

You took that and you put me to shame.

It's over and done with, for it's in the past.

I always knew me and you would never last.

The tears I cry, I cry for you.

You left me in misery and sorrow, too.

I can't take back the things I've said.

I can lay them down and put them to bed.

Anita Vaughn 1991

I Wish

I wish I may, I wish I might,
I wish you were someone in my life.
I wish I could be happy and enjoy life.
I wish I could understand, and be a caring wife.
I wish I had joy and lived a happy life.
I wish I may, I wish I might,
I wish you would be there, when I come out
And shine so bright.

Anita Vaughn 1991

Unspoken Truth

The Game

All this loneliness that has come down on me.
Because of your hurt and stupidity,
You left me hurting and so angry inside.
The only thing left, is just to say—goodbye.
Broken hearts and broken dreams,
Life was pictured with such a gleam.
When reality came into sight,
I knew from there on, it would be a hard fight.
Rainy days and cloudy skies,
Two people hurting in a lonely disguise,
Unnecessary hurt and unnecessary pain,
The lies that you told, were stupid and lame.
You told me your reasons and reasons why,
You couldn't stay with me, for it was all a lie.
You never loved me, for this you said:
I must bury my heart, for it's now dead.

Anita Vaughn 1991

Pass Me By

I always tried to be the perfect one for you.

In time you see, it just didn't do.

I gave you all I ever had.

You broke my heart and treated me bad.

I told you I'd always cry, until the day you pass me by.

Tears that fall from my eyes, pain and hurt from the lies,

I miss your tender touch, and oh, how I love you so much.

I said, that I would always stay near.

[In time] I knew you would disappear.

Now my heart, cries out for you.

Leaving me lonely, lonely and blue.

So, when you decide to pass me by,

Don't turn around, for there are no more good-byes.

Anita Vaughn 1991   Unspoken Truth

Feelings

I have this feeling, so deep in my soul,
It seems so complicated just to let go.
When we said our goodbyes, all I could do was cry.
You broke my heart and didn't care.
You left me with a loneliness I couldn't bare.
Though it was fun, now I regret for those days are done.
I miss you and this I must confess,
For you left my life an awful mess.
Now you say, you need me so?
After all that's happened; please, just go.
For my life with you could never be so.

Pain

When I close my eyes and squeeze them tight,
A memory of you brings a bright light.
It glows and shines and brings the tears.
All of a sudden, it brings back those years.
The scars and pain you brought to me,
Plain and in sight, so everyone could see
You hurt, cheated and lied,
You took all your feelings and put them aside.
You needed a certain untied love, with no tied
strings.
Not a push or a shove, you wanted to be free.
You had to be free in every way.
I knew my love wouldn't make you stay.

Anita Vaughn 1992   Unspoken Truth

When I

When I look outside and see all the leaves upon the ground,

A happy feeling just comes around.

A feeling so strong that no one could hold back.

When I see the sun shining, glowing down upon your face,

All my emotions for you, just fall into place.

When I sit in the window and look at the wonderful moon,

I could never be with you a moment too soon.

When I see those sparkling stars in the sky,

I realize that it will always be you and I.

When I see the snow, all pure and white,

I think of a bright fire to warm us through the night.

Cuddling by one another, we are the perfect lovers.

When I feel the rain fall upon my face.

Reminds me of all the hard times, we've had to put back in place.

But most of all, when I see love, I see you and I.

Hand and hand, walking along, with love growing so bright.

Written Expressions   Anita Vaughn 1992

A Valentine Wish

Valentines is a special day for you,
To share with someone you love.
Hand in hand, like the fit of a glove,
Two people sharing—one common love.
A Valentines' wish so far, but yet so near,
Wishing to be with someone you find so dear.
An empty waiting to be filled,
Someone special who has that feel,
Longing for that love, that use to be.
That special someone, I long for to see.
A Valentines' wish, I hope will come true.
A Valentines' wish, from me to you.

Anita Vaughn 1993   Unspoken Truth

Anchor & Guide

I go back in memory on this autumn night,
To mama's gentle hands, that held me so tight.
She always had time to mend my broken wings,
Give courage and hope like the magic of spring.
I can hear singing, as I go down memory lane.
See her joyfully doing chores, ignoring her own pain.
As leaves stir gently, I felt a bit sensitive inside,
As I long for the hand, that was my Anchor & Guide.

Anita Vaughn 1993

Love

Two people who share one common love,
Heart to heart from Heaven above.
Joy and pain, laughter and cries,
Never wishing to ever say goodbyes.
It's like two hearts, becoming as one,
Me and you under the falling sun.
Hand in hand, arm in arm,
The two of us with glowing charm.
Distant love, that seems so near,
A wonderful feeling to shed a tear.
Lonely souls, yet open hearts,
A feeling of two which will never part.

Anita Vaughn 1993   Unspoken Truth

Unknown

A mystery person brought to my attention,
Who is sweet and nice, which was mentioned.
An average guy, with an average girl,
Two people to have, in each other's world.
Long and short meaningful talks
Hand in hand, having wonderful walks,
Sharing things, that we never knew.
Opening our hearts, from me to you.

Anita Vaughn 1993

Bondage

When you left me, I was sad.
I knew that time would pass.
Pass till the next day, when I see your face.
The stars light up bright in outer space,
Bringing joy and happiness to a life full of mess.
I think some enjoyment would be the best bet.
The two of us both seeking the same,
Both our hearts still remained in chains.
Trying to be free, to fly in the wind.
But somehow, the pain seems to never end.

Anita Vaughn 1993   Unspoken Truth

Confusion

Sometimes pain, yet sometimes glory,
This is my sad, but very true story.
My boyfriend was there at one time or another.
He vanished from my heart and destroyed others.
The man inside him will never appear
The other side at a time that's so dear.
He hurt me you know, but I still love him so.
It's very hard, hard to explain,
I feel I'm always the one to blame.
He won't admit it, because he thinks it's a sin.
This is my story, so let's began.
Triangles and squares and in the center, my man.
Always out and trying to enter in,
I pull him in, with all his pain, but he always ends up
out again.
Why won't he stay and show me a way?
That he can love me everyday?
There are good times, but they end up bad.
When he leaves, he kisses me saying,
What a good time we've had.
I wish he was loving all of the time.
That will be when day and night combine.
I must go now and tuck myself in.
There's nobody there; again and again.

Written Expressions   Anita Vaughn 1993

Perfect Gentleman

When I first seen you, it was like a dream come true.

A perfect gentleman, just the one same as you.

Two hearts, becoming as one,

Me and you together, under the falling sun.

The way you carried yourself was so amazing.

My eyes stuck on you, so bright and gazing.

The perfect gentleman, I would soon get a chance to meet.

The perfect gentleman for me.

Me and you holding hands, walking along the ocean blue.

Moonlight shinning, cool breeze blowing inside of you and me.

Opening doors and holding out hands,

This perfect gentleman, I'm speaking of is my man.

Anita Vaughn 1994   Unspoken Truth

Essence of You

When we first met, it was like a dream come true.
You with me and me with you.
Bringing me comfort and joy, happiness not pain.
A beautiful summer day without the rain
Lifting me up, when I'm feeling down.
Someone who I love, having around.
Hand in hand, strolling through the park,
Sharing our love, within our hearts.
A perfect gentleman, sent from Heaven above,
To come and fill my life with love.
Everyone has someone special, someone so special and true.
But I have a essence and this is my Essence of You.

Anita Vaughn 3/13/1996

Section 2

A Collection of Songs

Section 2

Let Go and Let God (Song)

(Verse 1)

Move out of His way
He is more than capable to change my ways
A new creature in Christ
From the top of my head
To the bottom of my feet
Allow God to finish what He's started in me

Chorus

Let go and let God work
Give it over to Him and He'll work it out
Let go and let God work
Victory is coming for you in the end

(Verse 2)

Leave the past behind
Move forward in Him and renew your mind
Striving to be just like our God
Living life in His own image
God loves us all forever

Unspoken Truth

So all should aim for eternal living

Chorus

Let go and let God work
Give it over to Him and He'll work it out
Let go and let God work
Victory is coming for you in the end

 Anita Vaughn 06/18/2011

My Shield (Song)

(Verse 1)

Deep in my heart I know You are with me
Through all of my trials I know You're here
When things are down I know You are around
Lord, You are my shield

Chorus

Lord, You are my shield

My protector and my healer
Lord, You are my shield
My keeper and my friend
Lord, You are my shield

(Verse 2)

My protection from all hurt harm and danger
My joy in the time of my sorrow
My Alpha and Omega, my beginning and my end
Lord, You are my shield

Chorus

Lord, You are my shield
My protector and my healer
Lord, You are my shield
My keeper and my friend
Lord, You are my shield
Victory is coming for you in the end

Anita Vaughn 06/07/2011   Unspoken Truth

I Need You Lord (Song)

Chorus:

I need You, Lord
Today, tomorrow and forever more
I need You, Lord
To close and open doors

(Verse 1)

When my bills are do and no money to pay
Feeling closed in, can't find my way
Nobody understands, lost and having no direction
I need You, Lord just a glimpse of Your reflection

Chorus:

I need You, Lord
Today, tomorrow and forever more
I need You, Lord
To close and open doors

(Verse 2)

Can't do this alone. I need You by my side
With Your guidance and direction I won't go wrong
You have turned me around. I'm on the right path
Your blessings keep flowing. I'm happy and praying
that it will last

Written Expressions

Chorus:

I need You, Lord
Today, tomorrow and forever more
I need You, Lord
To close and open doors

(Verse 3)

Your love and presence in my life gives me total joy
Happiness and a feeling of eternal life with You
Lord, I thank You for my life. My ups outweigh my
downs
I thank You for being ever present in my life.

Chorus:

I need You, Lord
Today, tomorrow and forever more
I need You, Lord
To close and open doors

Section 3

Searching

Section 3

Hold On

The pain of life hurts so deep within,

No peace, no joy, nothing seems to end.

Back and forth, my mind is constantly moving.

The entire world, wants me to believe that I'm losing.

Fear comes upon me and I worry and wonder why?

Tears roll down my face, as I call to the Most High.

Help me Lord, for I am weak, vulnerable and lost.

Out He stretched His hands and says "I've paid the cost."

Stand my child and be strong in the Lord.

Fear and worry not, because the morning will have joy.

Trust me and believe, that I hear you and am with you.

Picture Me on the cross and know, that I'm near you.

Keep fighting my child and have faith that it's done.

Rejoice every second, because your battle is already won.

I Do

Communication is a must and seeking God is too.
For we stood before the Father and said I Do.
Commitment and trust, sunshine and rain
Love and happiness, sometimes headache and pain,
The ups and downs, the good and the bad,
Our vows we took, should never end sad.
For love outweighs it all and always prevails too.
I said it then and I'll say it again,
I love you and I still do.

Anita Vaughn 03/19/2016

The Inner Man

When you see me walking, with my head held high.

I'm thanking God for wiping the tears from my eyes.

The smile upon my face and the laughter from my lips,

My utterance of praise, to the One, Who has given me a gift.

The gift of life, for all to see; for, if you knew what I had been through,

You wouldn't want to be me.

You look at the outer man, but never take the time to see.

For the outer man is only an image for the world to see.

Look inside and you will see, the inner man whom God has created me to be.

Anita Vaughn 03/28/2016   Unspoken Truth

My Father's Love

Born with a silver spoon and nice things too.

So many people wondering how you are able to do you.

The whirlwind of life, twirling all around,

Satan on my trail, trying to get me down.

The appearance that I portray, with a smile on my face,

I am truly able to shine, because of God's grace.

Protection from His wings and Angels all around,

The worries of this world, will never get me down.

He always sits high and covers from above.

It's nothing like having my Father's Love.

Anita Vaughn 03/28/2016

The Hand of God

The hand of God is moving in my life.
So, I can let go of my misery and strife.
Through thick and thin, He never fails.
As He whispers to me—all is well.
Worry no more, your trouble is done.
Victory is yours, for through Me you have won.
Be strong and keep moving towards Me.
I will draw to you, as you draw to Thee.
Head held high and arms out wide,
For on the cross I hung and died.
My resurrection has come for you a new beginning.
Stay with Me and watch Me work out a good ending.

Anita Vaughn 04/03/2016   Unspoken Truth

A Mother's Love

Protection of her children is number one,

Loving, caring until all is done.

A mother's love, so pure and sweet, Indescribable and unique.

The care she has to cover her own.

Making sure nothing goes wrong.

That same love, is what God has for us.

If we can learn to let go and trust,

Trust in Him and He will come through,

Not only for you, but for your children too.

Hold on to His Word, believe and stand.

When your children leave from you, He has them in His hand.

A Mother's Love will never end.

Her children watch her life, and learn to win.

As they grow old and venture out in life,

You will see your reflection in them, as we strive to be like Christ.

Anita Vaughn 04/17/2016

Thank You

We met so many years ago and who knew?
One day God would have something for you to do.
To be a vessel of His Holy Word and Truth.
To help out a friend, who is trying to fight through.
Our timing was wrong and we didn't know,
That God already had a plan and ready to show.
The love of God came through you, so bright.
I was attracted to it and needed the light.
You fed me with the Word of God.
Prayed with me, at any time.
You blessed me, with your awesome knowledge.
You assured me, that I would follow.
Encouragement from you all around,
You always lifted me up and never put me down.
You are truly Heaven sent, and I thank Him for you.
Without you in my life, I wouldn't know what to do.
God, I thank you for Your servant on Earth.
For she has blessed me and showed me my worth.

Anita Vaughn 04/17/2016   Unspoken Truth

Who Are You?

Who are you? Not the one I've known so long.
Who Are You? Not the one who was so strong
So many years of a loving caring man...
To see you allow the devil to come in and take a
stand?
What happened to the one I married?
Is he lost and need to be carried?
Back to the way you used to be,
I need the old you to be set free.
I feel as if, I've been with a stranger.
Is this the real you? Have I been in danger?
Callused, evil, disrespectful and lust?
This is the one I cannot trust!
Who Are You? Will you ever return?
Who Are You? Not the one!

Anita Vaughn 04/17/2016

A Personal Relationship

I had to be hurt, to come fully to You.
I've always known You, but not what to do.
You've been here with me all along.
Your Word keeps making me very strong.
We sit and conversate as often as I like.
I get so excited, with all my might,
Your love is so precious and I need it now.
I've been drawing to You and now I know how.
My teachings have truly helped me out.
Without the Word I'm lost without a doubt.
I'm learning more of You and what is true.
I've come this far and I know it's because of You.
Our relationship has changed the past few months,
It's gotten stronger and stronger and over some humps.
Filled with the Holy Spirit, which leads and guides me.
I shine for Jesus for the entire world to see.
Now I feel Your presence and know that it's You.
No one can tell me now that I don't love You.
For my love is real and long over due.
A personal relationship that I have is so true.

Anita Vaughn 04/17/2016   Unspoken Truth

Thoughts

I have mixed emotions and I'm trying to deal,
[Often] asking myself: is this situation real?
So hard to believe that I'm in this place.
A broken heart, with so much empty space.
Negativity spoken to me and will it last?
Have I allowed some things to come from my past?
He comes to try and take me out.
My mind is going crazy, without a doubt.
There is a man I know, that can change this around.
Look to Him, seek Him and He will not let you down.
Fill my empty open space with all Your love.
Restore me, love me and open up Heaven above.
Renew my mind spirit soul and heart too.
For all the negativity, I know is not true.
I am a child of the Most High!
He who comes to destroy me, is definitely a lie.
Pushing forward to be who, I've been called to be.
Lord, please create in me a clean spirit and set me free.
I'm seeking Your face and crying out Your Name,
On my knee's before You, trying not to be shamed.

Written Expressions   Anita Vaughn 04/23/2016

Forgiveness

You made me believe, that the problem was me.

I was so hurt in my heart, that I couldn't see.

Your words you spoke so harsh and mean.

I tried to wake up, but it was not a dream.

You stood before me, so bold and sure,

You accepted the calling to be so pure.

I can't believe that this is really you.

I've been praying for you and I forgive you

I've loved you for so many years and now you're gone.

I can't seem to get the courage to pick up the phone.

It's almost as if, I'm scared to see you.

I use to always want to be near you.

Forgiveness is key and something that I must do.

To move on with life with or without you.

The hurt and pain you caused, you didn't want me to live.

But, I've found in my heart to forgive.

Anita Vaughn 04/23/2016   Unspoken Truth

Fear/Forward

Hurt to the core and can't see my way,
Depressed, loss of appetite, and crying all day.
Negative thoughts all through my mind,
Trying to figure out life and feel like I'm dying.
Fear of what will happen next,
No sleep, can't rest, and very stressed.
Trying to move forward, from all the hurt and pain.
Talking and praying, trying to stay sane.
Helpful friends sent from Heaven above,
Assuring me that it will get better with love.
Moving forward, [now] my main concern.
This was a very hard lesson that I had to learn.
Though I felt like dying and giving up too.
I knew that God would see me through.
Now I'm better and what can I say?
I look back on fear and I've moved forward today.

Anita Vaughn 07/26/2016

Second Chance

Years ago I thought he was the one.
Life came between us and we were done.
Seeing each other from time to time.
My thoughts of him flowing through my mind.
Years gone by and we both had moved on too,
A question in my head: Was our love true?
Doing my own thing and trying to get by,
Is the life I'm living, all a big lie?
I never thought I would be joined with him again.
Life has a strange way of making amends.
Now he's back and can this be real?
He's opened his heart and now I know the true deal.
[For years] I thought very negative of him.
Not knowing, that he was hanging out on a limb.
Have I deprived us both of what we could've been?
Holding on to negative things to the end.
A new opportunity has come my way.
I will make the best of it at the end of the day.
Starting all over, is such a big challenge.
God give me the strength to be open and see what
happens.

Anita Vaughn 07/25/2016   Unspoken Truth

Is It True?

Is it True? Does he love me as he says he do?

His actions are confusing and I'm still getting to know you

Is it True? Will we be together forever as his heart speaks out?

I sometimes feel as if he really loves me without a doubt

Is it True? Has he longed for me all these years?

His heart hurting and his eyes filled with tears?

Is it True? Has he matured to be a fine young man?

Opening doors, pulling out chairs and holding my hand.

Is it True? Our separate paths has given us character charm and a lesson well learned, to bring us back together into each other's arms.

Is it True? Have we always been one with each other and just didn't know what to do?

Anita Vaughn 07/26/2016

Section 4

Transformation

Section 4

Letting Go

Letting go of someone you love is a hard thing to do.

The hurt, the pain seems like you will never get through.

You reflect on yourself and think what did I do wrong?

Something comes to you and you realize you were losing yourself all along.

Your big heart and giving spirit has caused you a lot of pain and tears.

Now it has put you in a place of trying not to fear.

Hoping and praying that all your flaws will not leave you lonely.

You keep finding yourself back in this same moment.

Thoughts

Why am I back in this place?
Was it all just a show?
Does he really love me?
I miss him so.

Is it something wrong with me?
I don't want to be alone.
Will I ever be happy?
Or just disappear and be gone.

Can I support myself and live free?
Why would such hurtful things come against me?
I'm tired of being hurt by the ones I love.
Will I ever have a true relationship from above?

Sometimes I just want to give up and go.
I ask myself, is it worth it though?
Do I love him enough to work it out?
Only if it's done without a doubt.

Written Expressions   Anita Vaughn 10/07/2017

Who Am I?

When I look in the mirror, what do I see?

A woman who has had a good and rough life, but still holding on.

I cry, laugh, get sad and depressed sometimes, but yet still standing.

Wants love and wants to give love.

Scared of hurt, failure and pain.

Strong, giving, caring, very outspoken and closed all in the same.

Confused, happy and stressed but all in all still give my best.

Does this make me a bad person in some people's eyes?

I don't know but all I can be is who I am.

The Beginning

This is all new to you, but something I've already been through.

Together we can figure it out to make it last; because, it's so much better than the last.

Times when you think you have it all and then it all just falls.

Future is something, we all think about and dream about.

What will happen? What will we become? Will we be happy and become as one?

Ups and downs we all must go through. Keep the faith and God will see you through.

Love, Joy, peace and happiness are just a few. God will supply all your needs if you allow him to be in you.

Me

A beautiful baby girl, chocolate and sweet.
An innocent soul for the Lord to keep.
A toddler at 2, spoiled rotten who knew?

Now a little girl and time for school. A brilliant mind and so much to discover.

On to the teenage years with middle school and high. Singing, cheerleading and happy inside.

Graduation time is here and all will cheer. She made it this far with yet so much on her heart.

Touched as a younger child in a place not meant to be. Holding it inside because it was family.

Young adult wanting to be grown. Had a son and now he's gone. God called him home.

The hurt and pain she felt cannot be described. Shut down, running away and nowhere to hide.

Blessed with son #2 scared to death not knowing what to do.

Will he be okay she asked? Am I doing things right? He's all grown up now and such a sight.

In an abusive relationship beaten, battered and torn. She can't take anymore she wants to leave him alone.

The struggle she has is too much to bear. She took some pills to clear the air.

Unspoken Truth

Taking too many and now what to do? She ends up in the hospital under psychiatric care.

Finding out she's pregnant and trying to kill herself too. Lord help this young lady, for she is in despair.

A beautiful daughter, who saved her life has been her drive to keep living.

Marriage at 23 and had her ups and downs. A successful business owner and helpful all around.

Who would have guessed the perfect marriage in everyone's eyes would end abruptly and ruin lives.

Pain and hurt again as she figures things out. She stuck with God and it all worked out.

Still dealing with the remnants of all that mess, has made her a better woman, than she laid to rest.

Now in a new place in life, struggling to move forward and have a good life.

A new relationship and don't know how to deal with it. Is she to set in her ways to handle it?

Will it last or fall apart too? Is she ready for that or has she not had time to really deal with the true self?

Mother

Most beautiful inside and out,
On top of her game, without a doubt.
The one her children look up to,
Her heart and love shines, through and through.
Eager to help and always there too,
Rejoicing to have a mother—just like you.

HAPPY MOTHER'S DAY

Anita Vaughn 05/12/2019   Unspoken Truth

Transformation

As you look out onto a tree you find a cocoon rolled tightly.
Patiently waiting to be exposed, the questions of what? Why? No one knows.

A few weeks later, it's time to be set free.
Wings of beautiful color and distinct markings.
A new world with a different look.
Sounds like a transformation of the Good Book.

We all have been in a worldly cocoon.
Trapped, scared and tightly wound.
Weeks, months and even years we cannot be found.

Then [one day] we began to break free.
Learning more of the Word and becoming me.
Distinctive characteristics and markings too.
God has created a new creature in you.

All so blessed, to become who we should be. The transformation if for the world to see.

Anita Vaughn 06/02/2019

The Truth About You

When you ask God to show you yourself, be prepared for nothing less.

You will have all sorts of emotions. Thinking: am I really this person?

It will hurt and sometimes make you feel a certain way. All in all, just accept it and start to pray.

God can change you, if you allow Him to. It's hard to hear the truth about you.

Reflect on your answers and think it through. God will not steer you wrong, only you.

When you look in the mirror, it's hard to see. You're looking at the outer man when you should look inside and be free.

Free from all that you've heard from years ago to now. You have been shown yourself and it's true.

God has revealed the truth about you.

A Man

Teach me how to love You.
Teach me how to be true.
I'm speaking of a man,
No God, that man is You.

You will always love me.
You will always be loyal and faithful too.
You won't tell me lies because Your Word is true.

Hold me and rock me in Your arms.
Be by my side through and through.
This man I speak of God, is You.

A friend, provider, lawyer and doctor,
A real true man and a protector too.
An amazing God, with so much to feel.
It's almost unbelievable the love you give.

What a powerful person and some don't understand
The man you have may be amazing, but my God is
a real true man.

Anita Vaughn 06/11/2019

Section 5

Expressions

Section 5

My Child

When you raise a child and do all that you can do.

Lots of questions arise, one being: will they make it through?

The long days and tiring nights.

A good mother will never give up her fight.

The conversations some hard and some a must.

Will my child grow and learn to trust?

Trust the one who can give them all.

The one who blessed me with you and I trust in him to never let you fall.

I've made mistakes and regret them so.

I've repented of my sins and now it's time to grow.

Grow into what I should already be.

He's been by my side and never left me.

They have gone through life with lots of ups and downs.

I wanting to help but they are all grown now.

Still trying to protect them and keep them safe.

I can advise as much as possible but it's their own race.

Wishing I could catch them before making big mistakes.

Lord let my child one day look to you and seek your face.

Anita Vaughn 06/24/2019   Unspoken Truth

My Black is Beautiful

My smooth dark skin and my plump full lips,
God didn't bless me with hardly any hips.
My full wide nose and thick hair too,
A lot of people wish to look like you.
The intelligence that I possess and the style, in which I dress.
My glasses on my face, I'm proud to be in the African American race.
My black is beautiful in so many ways, from my hair to my toes,
From my brain, to my soul.
It's not all what you see on the outside.
I'm very powerful, for what I possess on the inside.
Business minded and so many dreams to pursue
My black is beautiful, in and out too, boo.
From my strong voice and the talent of writing from heart to hand.
My black is beautiful and I now take a stand.
When you look in the mirror and realize what you see,
Your black is beautiful, so take hold of it just like me.

Anita Vaughn 06/11/2019

Elevation

Your elevation is on the other side of your exit.
If it's not a good choice, don't mess with it.
Things come and things go,
A seasonal change as it all flows.
When you exit out you began to see,
The elevation of the level you were meant to be.
Elevation can take you higher and higher.
But make sure you are not in the fire.
Fire will keep you down and not easily removed.
Don't allow things and people to keep you there, just refuse.
Once your fire is out and you finally see through the smoke.
Now you can rise to your elevation level with all hope.

Anita Vaughn 06/11/2019   Unspoken Truth

Dear God

It's me again, Your child whom You created.

I've tried to do things my way and should have just waited.

Waited on You to show me the way.

My controlling issue, definitely got in the way.

I've put man before You, to try and have a good life.

I look at my life [now] and see it was all a lie.

Years of pain, heartache and loss too;

All, because of the real me of anger, jealousy, envy,

Bitterness, money hungry, insecurity, negativity, and just being a fool.

Dear God, I repent before You on fallen knee,

Asking for Your forgiveness and to please change me.

Cleanse my heart and renew my soul, for age is just a number. But

I'm 48 years old.

When I asked You to show me myself. I was not prepared for the image I had left.

It's not of You and wrong; in so many ways.

I must make things right before the end of my days.

Dear God, I asked myself how can you be this way and still claim to be a Christian?

My answer came and said I've been trying to get your attention but you didn't listen.

I've had to allow things to come and go, some you took heed to and some no.

You are my child and I forgive you always

Now you are alone and we can start the process to do things my way.

You're hurting and going through right now.

You're wondering how you will come out of this somehow.

Be still my child and know I haven't left you yet and I will never go.

Anita Vaughn 06/11/2019   Unspoken Truth

Broken Hearted

So many broken pieces not knowing what to do.
I'm crying out to You, Lord; because I need you.
I need to hear You and feel Your love.
Distractions all around, I can't see Heaven above.
Fear, depression, and ungodly thoughts,
They cloud my mind, for my broken heart has me lost.
Focusing on Your Word and seeing Your face,
Please open my heart, and fill it with grace.
I know I'm here for a reason and it will all show.
I have to release my past and let it go.
I look to the hills, which cometh my help.
All along knowing, I have been kept.
You've been by my side this entire time.
Showing up in different ways, even when I'm crying.
My love for You has grown and I have so much to give.
My broken heart is not too much for You to heal.

Anita Vaughn 07/11/2019

Scared to Love

My past won't allow me to open up,
Scared to love and give another any trust.
Will they hurt my heart and cause me pain?
I don't know if I can withstand the rain!
Broken people have very sharp edges.
Sometimes we end up startled and bleeding in messes.
I have a wound still healing from recent words.
That cut like a sword, all the way down to the bone.
I cried out to You, Lord and I know You're here.
I feel Your presence and know You're near.
Scared to love and it end in pain,
Looking at self, and placing blame.
But there is beauty in the battle of love.
God is the perfect example from Heaven above.

Anita Vaughn 07/11/2019   Unspoken Truth

Be Still and Know

Trying to stay focused and do the right thing,
Knowing God is beside me and I won't complain.
Be still and know, that He's working it all out.
He won't let you down, just trust and not doubt.
He's paved the way for all of us to succeed.
Open your eyes, look around and believe.
It can be hard to be still and to do nothing.
But have patience and faith to trust Him.
Be still and know, that you have a sovereign God.
Willing and able to help you beat all odds.
Your life can be great, if you choose that path.
Be still and know, that God will always outlast.

Anita Vaughn 07/16/2019

I Loved You Enough, To Let You Go

What I thought was your love for me,

Turned out to be a mirage, that I couldn't see.

My love for you was deep and true.

It blinded me, from seeing the real you.

I've given my heart to you 100%.

To find out that we were never meant.

Stepping back and looking at our show,

I loved you enough to let you go.

Focusing on self and realizing my worth,

God has given me a purpose, right here on Earth.

Thoughts changing in a more positive way,

Finding happiness and I didn't think I would see the day.

So much devastation in my life, from being with you.

Often wondering: will I find a love that's true?

I loved you enough, to let you go.

I'm moving forward and just taking it slow.

Anita Vaughn 07/21/2019   Unspoken Truth

Caged No More

Behind bars and can't get out,
Looking through the cracks, screaming and shouting,
Feeling caged in, and so much on my mind.
Will I be able to break free? It's a matter of time.
Being told what to do and feeling less of myself,
I need some peace and love to set me free.
Now I'm out and caged no more.
I can express my gratefulness and soar.
Like the eagles flying high in the sky,
I can never reach my heights, if I don't try.
No more being put down and made to blame,
I'm my own person now and not looking for fame.
It feels so good to be open and at peace.
I am who I am, and I'm not afraid to speak.
My chains are being broken and the weight is much less,
I'm caged no more and striving for my best.

Losing Myself

I use to be happy and able to be free.
I find myself becoming less of me.
Losing myself for others to be happy.
I can't understand why I would be nagging.
The things that were so dear to me,
I've put on hold, to try and get security.
Reaching not one goal of my own,
To cater to someone, who was all wrong.
Losing myself in the midst of all the chaos and confusion,
My life is a mess and I feel like I'm losing.
Why would I do such a thing against myself?
If my eyes would've been opened, I would've left.
Eyes wide shut and feeling like I have no help.
The Lord was always with me, while I chose to lose myself.

Anita Vaughn 07/21/2019   Unspoken Truth

Section 6
It Is Written

Section 6

A Glimpse

Fill me with Your Holy Spirit, so my heart will be pure and true.

Striving hard to resemble just a glimpse of You.

Distractions all around and it's so hard to see,

Please lift me up Lord and wash me.

Never thought the tears would go away.

I'm much happier now and I give You all the praise.

Never thought I would feel again and see a pain free day.

I thank You Lord, because You made a way.

Breathe into me, so that my heart is pure before You.

You've changed my situation, my heart and soul too.

I give You all praise, honor and glory.

For this is just a little glimpse of my story.

It's All Necessary

The struggle, the pain, the heartache, the rain,
The ups and downs, the devil all around.

> —It's all necessary

The things we go through are not for us.
Our pain and burdens can help others trust.
He won't put more on us, than we can bear.
Our obstacles are all necessary to get us there.
We are all different, but all must go through.
If we trust in God, He will show us what to do.
When we come out, better than before,
We can know, He's opening doors.

> —It's all necessary

What we've been through and come out of
God was by our side, and showed us much love.
The pressure, the loneliness and being ashamed,
It was all necessary, so let's praise His Name.

Anita Vaughn 06/25/2019

You Can't Tell Me

You can't tell me, that God doesn't sit high and look low.

You can't tell me, that He won't cleanse you white as snow.

You can't tell me, that He doesn't love me so.

You can't tell me, that He will turn His back on me.

You can't tell me, that He won't set me free
I know Him personally.

You can't tell me, that He didn't rescue me.

You can't tell me, that He didn't take my pain away

You can't tell me, that He won't bring brighter days.

You can't tell me, that He isn't always there.

You can't tell me, that He will put more on me than I can bear.

I know Him personally.

You can't change my mind.

You can't tell me, anything negative about God because I know it's—a lie!

He Knows

He knows your sorrows, He knows your pain,
God will rescue us if we call on His Name.
Your life can be made whole again,
Stand firm in His Word and stake your claim.

He knows everything about you, from big things to small.
He is the Creator and created you; after all.
He knows when you're sad and need to be set free.
He gave His life for you and me.

He knows what you will do, before you do it.
He has paved the way for all of us to get through it.
When it seems like it's all falling down,
Remember our God is always around.
When you can't see past the hurt and pain,
Just be patient and call on His Name
He Knows!!

Anita Vaughn 06/27/2019

Thank You

I love you too:

I know you're hurting and in much pain. They say love is hard and ours will never be the same. I know you won't forget me for all that I've done. I truly believed that you were the one. Regret on your behalf will hold you back. Trying to keep up this image and it's all an act. Ego so big that it wouldn't let you be. Disrespectful, dishonest and never about me. Can't admit guilt for too much pride. I didn't think you would hurt me; I was always on your side. Now our love is gone and what we've built too. You act as if it's nothing but you gave it up and ruined it too. Dreams and prayers for someone like me. You were blessed with my type and didn't know what to do with me. Scared of love and afraid of what you could have. I know you loved me and it was genuine enough to last. You never meant to hurt me but felt you didn't deserve me. I won't forget about you and you will see me happy. You thought I was better off without you and I hope you reach your destiny.

The tears I have shed will not be the last. The pain I have inside will soon be in the past. So I thank you, thank you for pushing me into this woman to become pure free and true.

Unspoken Truth

78

I often wondered did you ever see the woman I was. The woman taking care of you and holding you down in love.

You were my heart and soul and I allowed you to taint my being. I didn't know then, but now I know the reason. So unequally yoked and blind by love. It took you doing me wrong to hear from Heaven above.

The tears I have shed, will not be the last. The pain I have inside will soon be in the past. So I thank you, thank you for pushing me into this woman to become pure free and true.

I know she will never be able to take my place and elevate you to a new level. You left me thinking I was less of a woman, but I know better.

You were my heart and soul and I allowed you to taint my being. I didn't know then, but now I know the reason. So unequally yoked and blind by love. It took you doing me wrong to hear from Heaven above.

The tears I have shed, will not be the last. The pain I have inside will soon be in the past. So I thank you, thank you for pushing me into this woman to become pure free and true.

Life will teach you how to survive and I hope you're

happy. This chapter is closing in my life. God closes doors that no man can open. Thank you for walking out on what we built together. It has been spoken.

The tears I have shed, will not be the last. The pain I have inside will soon be in the past. So I thank you, thank you for pushing me into this woman to become pure free and true.

First Love

My first love was so long ago. The remembrance of his love is like yesterday, though. Always around each other and so in love too. We talked about marriage and everyone knew. The good times we shared and the future we planned. Ended up wrong and not in God's hands.

We moved on in our lives in our own ways. Sitting and reflecting back on all the good days. It wasn't meant to be then and that we now know. Our first son passed away and we were definitely through.

The hard times we had from our loss. Depressed, running and life is just a toss. Trying to move forward in our life. I've now left my first love to become a wife.

26 years of my first love being gone. I look up and find him back on my phone. Being the man I needed him to be. Always there with a listening ear to comfort me.

For now, I am no longer a wife, but a free woman; indeed. My first love saw an opening to try and meet my needs. Years went on and all was well at first. He began to show his true colors and it hurt.

Was I a fool now to be twice? He was gone for 26 years and now back in my life. My eyes were wide shut because I loved him so. God came in and said "I must let him go"

It's harder to walk away, when you love what's killing you. I think all in all, I already knew. He's my first love.

Unspoken Truth

Kryptonite

Kryptonite is known as something that can seriously weaken or harm a particular person or thing. My kryptonite is a man and I won't call his name.

His lifestyle is so exciting and he seems to have it all together. He says the right things and does the right things, to make it all better. Be careful though. Kryptonite will ease you in slow.

His charm and smooth talk will have you feeling some type of way. He calls and texts at the right time of day. His appearance so clean and debonair too. He knows he looks good and makes you feel good too.

Kryptonite will weaken your heart and state of mind. You fall in love and think it's just a matter of time. Time for him to choose just only you. Remember its kryptonite and it's not love boo.

He breaks your heart over and over again. You keep going back because, it's calling your name. You know it's all wrong and you try to get out. Kryptonite weakens your state and you can't seem to get out.

One day you finally wake up after all that has gone

on. To find you beaten, battered, and torn. You look around and kryptonite is gone. He's had his run with you and left you all alone.

Be very careful when dealing with this thing. It comes to kill steal and destroy and leave you with no dreams.

Unspoken Truth

Is He Real?

Showing affection and attentive to my needs.
Lord help me to soften my heart and receive.
Receive him rubbing my face and holding my hand.
I didn't think there was such a man,
I have prayed and cried for someone like him.
Thoughts in my mind saying, Is He Real?
So much in common, that I get nervous to speak.
He's in my mind and this is all too deep.
Knowing what he wants and can articulate it to me.
I know I prayed for this but can it be?
Did he finally arrive, after all I've been through?
Did God send this man and will he be true?
His head is on straight with ambitions and he has goals.
We seem to be compatible, but only God knows.
Is He Real?

Anita Vaughn 07/11/2019

Section 7
A Work In Process

Section 7

Patience For The Process

Changing times and situations too,
Having patience for the process, is a very hard thing to do.
Wanting things now and not seeing anything new,
Thoughts going through your mind, wondering, will I make it through?

Family and friends giving you all the love and support.
Worldly signs trying to make you feel like you can't take any more.
Satan's very busy trying to keep you the same,
You, on your knees crying out in Jesus' Name.

Knowing the process, is what you need to go through.
You ask God, to please give you patience and a new you.
The process can be painful and necessary at the same time.
Just open your heart and keep God on your mind.

Be still and know that God is working it out for your good.

Unspoken Truth

Stand firm on His Word and watch as we all should.
No need to help and put ourselves in the way,
Have patience for the process and be put on display.

Not for glory nor for fame,
But to show patience, for the process and edify Jesus' Name.

Beauty For Ashes

When you've gone through the storm
And everything is all torn down,
God will step in and turn it all around.

When your life seems dim and you can't see through the smoke,
Be blessed in what you have, take a stand and hope.

Beauty for Ashes after all has burned down;
Stop, look and see that God never let you down.

Blowing in the breeze, you can see it all fade away.
God is by your side; each and every day.

The trials we face, can make us want to lose our fight.
We must stand and be bold, with all our might.

When we come through our struggles with our heads held high;
Just remember, He blessed you with Beauty For Ashes.

Now just live your life

Anita Vaughn 08/15/2019   Unspoken Truth

Nothing Just Happens

Nothing just happens in life. It's all a part of God's plan.

Be strong and hopeful. Put your hand in his hand.

We look at our lives and often wonder why.

Jesus paid the price for us to call to the Most High.

Some try to plan their life to be what they see.

God has a plan and it will come to be.

We fight and struggle to do what we must.

Nothing just happens, we need to learn to trust.

Our paths are already laid out for us to go on,

God has sent several signs to show us our own.

Despite our roads and challenges we make,

Our path has been made and getting to it is not too late.

Nothing just happens and you will see,

The plans I had for my life, didn't fit me.

Anita Vaughn 08/15/2019

My Squad

Different positions and different things to do,
A squad is a team, that helps you pull through.

They know your plans and what needs to be done,
With everyone in place, the battle is already won.

Practice to perfection and all know what to do,
My squad has my back and we can't lose.

A powerful squad made from Heaven for you,
He's placed everyone in position, and you never knew,

They fall in place and you don't have to say a thing,
God has already confirmed what each must bring.

When the end is near and you see the end,
Remember your squad; because, collectively you win!

Anita Vaughn 09/17/2019   Unspoken Truth

Past to Present

Way back in the day, without a worry in the world,
Having fun just trying to be boys and girls.
Things start to change and growing up too,
So many challenges not knowing what to do.
Your ups and downs mold you into who you will be.
God watches over you, for only He can see.
Different stages that we all must learn from and go through.
His love has kept us protected and maintained.
We fall to our knees, because we can't stand the pain.
From past to present and we are all grown up now.
Looking back and thanking him for getting us here somehow.
Past pops up in the present and we ask what do we do?
Lord give me direction and strength to make it through.
The enemy will fool you and let your past shimmer and shine.
But God is looking upon me and saying "No Satan, she's mine".

Anita Vaughn 09/17/2019

Dark World

The world is full of deception, smoke and mirrors,

Delusions of the enemy to keep you from hearing.

It may be someone you love or someone you just met.

Maybe a past fling, don't get caught in the net.

Distractions all around to keep you from seeing his face.

Press forward bold and strong and take your place.

The enemy can't destroy you unless you fall.

Put your hand in the Master's hand, look forward and know,

The enemy is real and will take everything from you.

Trust God, lean on Him and He'll see you through.

The harder evil comes, the more you need to pray.

Throw your hands up, I rebuke you is all you need to say.

Call out to God and watch Him work.

Keep your mind stayed on Him and the devil will not lurk.

Resist him and he will flee, just call to God and take a knee.

Anita Vaughn 09/17/2019   Unspoken Truth

Change Me

As usual Lord I end up in this place, stumbling along trying to find my space.
I feel like I won't make it to see another day, change me Lord, so I can find my way.

I'm crying out to You, to free me from self.
Deliver me, hold me, for I am a mess.
Stuck in bondage from the past, feeling guilt and shame; because nothing last.

Reach down Lord and take my hand, help me love me and be able to stand.
Change me Lord, to be who I was called to be.
I'm humble before you on bending knee.

You formed me to be all I was created to be.
Help me Lord for I desire to be free
Change me Lord because only You can, I surrender my will.
Please, take me by the hand.

Anita Vaughn 09/23/2019

Work For It

When you work for my love, you will see,
All the work you put in was worth receiving me.
I'm a one of a kind diamond, which is hard to find.
It's not just my looks, but a powerful mind.
I'm not perfect and I will never claim to be.
You will understand my worth, just wait and see.
If I allow any and everything to come my way.
I will never have peace, not even for one day.
"Why work hard at it?" some may ask.
If you don't, I guarantee that it won't last.
When you use all your energy, resources and financ-
es too.
What you receive will be very special and important
to you.
If it's handed to you and everything is easy and free,
As I said earlier, it won't last, just trust me.
Put in work to show me, you want me and care.
Remember, God won't put more on you than you
can bear.

Anita Vaughn 09/26/2019   Unspoken Truth

Free Me

I did everything to make it work, but I'm still at a loss.

I keep having to remind myself to let it go, because You died on the cross.

No one can heal me, deliver me or set me free.

I'm calling out to You daily, kneeling on one knee.

The tears of knowing, that I've failed You again and again.

If I could just sit myself down, I know I would win.

Trying to do things my way and make them work out,

Lord, I've over stepped my boundaries without a doubt.

Free me from myself and all the pain I've caused.

For without You by my side, I will remain lost.

Anita Vaughn 10/09/2019

2 Faces

The outer face #1 so beautiful and so bright, an amazing smile full of light.

Appearance of a well groomed person, well put together; but still hurting.

When you look at her, all you can see, such a stunning woman; striving to be.

Putting on this face, #1 for people to see, Face #2 will truly shock thee.

She hides #2 so, and keeps it under wraps, when she arrives home—tears fill her lap.

The inner face #2 is no match for #1, #2 can only be helped by God's Son.

So much guilt, pain, and hurt she carries around, this #2 is so hard to be found.

2 faces in one beautiful hurting woman, [one day] will merge and no one will be able to keep her under.

Anita Vaughn 10/09/2019   Unspoken Truth

98

Crazy Faith

Faith the size of a mustard seed, is all you need.

Trust Him, call out to Him, if you please.

Crazy faith is what I desire and strive for.

No wavering or distractions, can't see it but want more.

Faith is the substance of things hoped for and the evidence of things not seen.

My crazy faith I desire, will push me beyond my means.

Stepping out and knowing that I know He has my needs.

No matter what the world may bring up and say,

My faith will always remind me, that He will make a way.

Faith, crazy faith or any kind of faith is what we need.

Small or big, put your trust in God and see.

Section 8

More Revealed

Section 8

Self Destruction

Sometimes we feel as if things are good.

We look at what we think we see and never understand.

Our tongues are brutal, and we didn't even know.

Self destruction followed, because out of the mouth it flowed.

Our thoughts of ourselves can be damaged all along.

Our minds in a place of thinking all wrong.

We hear all the things that people say about us.

Not realizing we should listen to God. That's a must!

To destroy we can bomb, demolish or even tear down,

This can happen even when no one's around.

Self destruction is sometimes realized and sometimes not.

We are in our own way and should turn it over to God.

Once you've realized that you are in the way,

Get down on your knees and began to pray.

Ask for His guidance and to move you out the way.

Open your heart and ears and listen to what He has to say.

Anita Vaughn 11/17/2019   Unspoken Truth

One Wing

A beautiful eagle flying up in the sky,

Wind blowing and he's gliding by his wings; so high.

He soars above all other birds, because he's made with special abilities.

Vision for far off sight to see prey and to feed.

Precision in all the things he was made to do and does.

Made by the most high God from Heaven above.

Imagine if one wing was gone and things changed tremendously.

The special gifts, would no longer be his abilities .

One wing clipped and all has changed.

Trust God at this point, because he never changed!

Our minds began to wonder and Satan is on his way in.

One wing has changed some things, and we now think we can't win.

Sometimes life throws us ups and downs.

The eagle's wing may be clipped, but healing is around.

Look up to Heaven and seek His face.

One wing won't keep you grounded in this place

Anita Vaughn 11/17/2019

Purpose or Preference

The decisions we make and the life we live,
Is it our purpose or presence for God's will?
Our purpose, is what we are called to do in life.
Some know what that is and some still fight.
Our preference, is what we chose to do on our own.
Nothing of God and usually end up all wrong.
Purpose or preference is an easy choice for some
Lifestyle, love, and background we already know the one.
Fulfill your purpose and everything else will come.
Trust God know and believe that He's the One.
Walk in your purpose and live in it too.
Move away from your preference and God will see you through.

Anita Vaughn 11/17/2019   Unspoken Truth

Divine Delays

God will delay our path, to reach our destiny.
His love for us will keep us pressing,
Divine delays are not necessarily a bad thing,
We all have them, but we all don't take heed.
Our paths are laid out from before we were born.
By the Trinity of 3—Holy Spirit, Father and Son.
Look watch and listen to the Voice from up above.
He is always with us, and showers us with love.
Divine Delays or delays we bring on ourselves,
A necessary road in life; to keep from going left.
Trust your path, look forward and straight,
Your Divine Delays will definitely be worth the wait.
Growth in life from all you've gone through.
Praying to God saying, I know You have me too.

Anita Vaughn 11/24/2019

Don't Fight It

You're told you're nothing and you should be ashamed.

Jesus died on the cross and took all the blame.

People see you and know that you have changed.

But they can't let the new you shine; because of your past games.

Don't fight it and just let it be.

He has already paid the price for you and me.

Some will see your change and some will not want to.

You've prayed, cried and grown, now stand strong and be free.

Mistakes you have made, you have learned from and moved on.

Don't fight against what people say, but some may do you wrong.

Talk about you behind your back and smile in your face.

Don't fight it, keep moving forward, trying not to repay.

God will be your vindicator, if you just take your place.

Anita Vaughn 11/26/2019   Unspoken Truth

Uproot It

Deeply rooted in my soul, are things not of God and I have no control

Please cleanse me, wash me and make me whole.

Insecurity, no trust, low self-esteem just to name a few.

A lonely heart, crazy past and can't seem to make it through.

Uproot it all and place it at His feet.

Guilt hurt and shame, I give to You Lord, please release me.

When I'm alone I scream, take it out of me if it's not of You!

God has been waiting on me to get my breakthrough.

Uproot it all and plant something new.

Water it, send the sun down and watch it bloom.

You give us all we need to live a blessed and prosperous life.

Uproot it all, make us new; so we may keep You in sight.

I can't do it by myself without You on my side.

I lay it all at Your feet; even my stubbornness and pride.

Written Expressions   Anita Vaughn 11/27/2019

Purchased Love

You were good for me when I was broken.

Not good for me while I'm whole?

I purchased your love to sooth my soul

Giving all that I had with money love and time

Knowing in my heart to you it was all about the dime

It's hard to make a good pick of a mate, when you are in a bad place.

God has greatness for you, but the wrong things are in its space.

A purchased love is something that can be easily let go; when the benefits leave

The receiver walks out and the buyer ends up pleading.

You find yourself to rather be stuck and safe than be progressive and vulnerable.

So you purchase love, to have someone to be up under.

Don't purchase love and they end up in the breeze.

Jesus purchased our love on the cross and it was given to you for free.

Anita Vaughn 12/10/2019   Unspoken Truth

Acting Out of Emotions Will Cost You

Anger, harsh words and physical harm will all cost you if you don't control them.

Stop, think and pull it together, handing it all over to him.

God is your vindicator and He will repay.

Acting out of emotions will cost you more than you are willing to pay.

A 5 second delay can change an outcome from bad to good.

Just take a second and think, because no one thought you would.

Emotions are tough and can be controlled:

Get your thought together and take a hold.

You ask yourself: would I rather deal with the pain of loneliness and brokenness too?

Look to God, for He will see you through.

Trust Him, seek Him and take that pause;

Because, acting out of emotions will cost you it all.

Section 9

Truths

Section 9

Thank You for the Steps

Steps have different levels and our lives do too.
I thank you for the steps that I've had to go through.
We [often] want to be at the top and to be seen.
God has it all planned out, to wash us and make us clean.
Our steps are ordered and that we must see,
Open our hearts and mind, to stay on bending knee.
All steps are not the same; in size, shape, color or depth.
Our life determines our stride to see our help.
Thank you for the steps of my life, which were necessary for me.
Continue to guide my steps, so I can see.
This journey that I'm on, is one long overdue.
Thank you God; because, I couldn't do it without You.

Purpose in the Pain

The pain so deep, that you feel numb inside.

Moving through life as if, you have nothing to hide.

The weight of your world pressing down on your shoulders.

Please Lord, let her know that You are there to hold her.

There is purpose in the pain that we all go through.

It strengthens us, develops us and grows us too.

Life without pain at some point in time,

Would make us keep on doing what we do, until we are dying.

No change, no different, and we would feel as we didn't need God.

The purpose in the pain, is it draws us closer to our Lord.

Pain can make you want to give up on life.

Remember God the Father and keep on fighting.

Anita Vaughn 01/11/2020

No Greater Love

As I grew older, I began to see the love that I thought would come to me.

All the movies and songs that sound so good and true.

To later come to see, that there is no greater love than God has for me.

From my good to my bad, my flaws and my truths.

The love I speak of: is unconditional, and will never leave you sad or blue

Forgiveness, everlasting and always by your side,

The kind of love that you don't ever want to hide.

Everyone should experience this kind of love.

No greater love, than the One from above.

Dry your eyes and look to the sky.

The greatest love you'll ever know, is from the Most High.

Anita Vaughn 01/16/2020   Unspoken Truth

Battle in Your Mind

Thoughts running rampant in your head,
Can't eat, can't sleep, trying to be spiritually fed.
Satan on his job, with distractions all around;
Remember, you are a child of God and stand your ground.
Don't get stuck and lose the battle in your mind.
Focus on God and He will not leave you behind.
Your mind is your power and your power is your mind.
Keep your hand to the plow, keep moving ahead and don't look back this time.
The battle in your mind is one of the enemy's.
He comes to steal, kill and destroy; so, stay on your knees.
Control your thoughts with positive and good.
Study your Word, seek God and pray as you should.
A battle in your mind is a hard thing to go through.
Trust God, hear His Voice and become the best you.

Anita Vaughn 01/27/2020

It's Time to Live

Holding back goals and doing for all that I love.
I'm thankful for life and blessings from up above.
Putting self last, but happy in all that I've done.
Looking back at my history and the race that I've run.
I have been breathing and now it's time to live.
A promising future and so much to give.
Older and wiser; I've gone through a lot of tests.
I hear a soft Voice saying: you must still press.
So much life left for me to live and just be.
Open my horizon for the entire world to see.
Coming out from my past and willing to be me,
It's time for me to live; so God, please set me free!

Anita Vaughn 02/03/2020   Unspoken Truth

Good to Greatness

When your life is all together and things are going good.

You sometimes forget how you got to the place you are, but never should.

We let the counterfeit of being good, stop us from our greatness.

We are content with good, when we were built for greatness.

We are more than conquers and can be whatever we choose.

Go from good to greatness; because, you have nothing to lose.

It may be a risk and tough times too.

Our Father formed you and knows you can make it through.

Nothing comes easy and if it does,

Step back, take a good look and make sure it's from above.

Go from good to greatness and share your story.

The entire world will see God's glory.

Epilogue

This particular book has been a great inspiration for me to write. It details my life's history from good to bad and everything in between. It was a bit of a struggle at times for me to read, because it placed me back in some situations that I had been in.

God has transformed my mind and heart through this experience, so that I am able to share a little bit of me with you. I have been sad, happy, moved, blessed and transparent. I have seen much growth with this book.

Everyone can relate to at least one piece in my book. As you are reading you will began to see the move of God in my life as I progressed on. I pray that it will transform you as it has me.

Be Blessed

Anita Vaughn

Enjoy these other great books from
Bold Truth Publishing

EFFECTIVE PRISON Ministries
by Wayne W. Sanders

Friendly Evangelism
by Barbara Walker Sowersby

KINGDOM of LIGHT 1 - kingdom of darkness
Truth about Spiritual Warfare
by Michael R. Hicks

GUIDELINES - PRAYING for the Sick
by Dr. Marilyn Neubauer

MENE, MENE, TEKEL, UPHARSIN
Thou art weighed in the balances, and art found wanting - Daniel 5:27
PROPHETIC POETRY FOR THESE PERILOUS END-TIMES
by Marcella Burnes

FIVE SMOOTH STONES
by Aaron Jones

SPIRITUAL BIRTHING
Bringing God's Plans & Purposes into Manifestation
by Lynn Whitlock Jones

PITIFUL or POWERFUL?
THE CHOICE IS YOURS
by Rachel V. Jeffries

Available through Bold Truth Publishing, select bookstores, and Amazon.com

Made in the USA
Middletown, DE
22 March 2020

86967624R00076